it shouldn't happen to a .... Christian

Special Dedication

I want to dedicate this book to Freda Brazier, I call her a 'soldier', and that she is, a true 'soldier of the cross' in every sense of the word.

Peter and Freda Brazier have travelled the length and breadth of the British Isles and many places overseas when most other people would think of putting on their slippers and retiring, such was their passion.

My lasting memory of Freda was in 1992 in the Philippines way up in the mountains, some 7 hours beyond Baggio. After badly damaging her leg in a fall, yet never missing a meeting and in fact insisting that we carry her in so that she could teach in the sessions she was allotted, because that is what, as she would say, "I came to do".

Oh I neglected to say, some of us call her 'mummy Freda' because of the overwhelming care and concern she had for others in the ministry.

Now laid low through illness, I want to say, and I am sure merely echo the thoughts of others, Freda, I salute you.

it shouldn't happen to a .... Christian

by Gary Stevenson

Barratt Ministries Publications

It Shouldn't Happen To A ... Christian
by Gary Stevenson

British Library Cataloguing-in-Publication Data
A catalogue record for this book is available from the British Library

ISBN: 0 9528222 6 1

Published 2002 by Barratt Ministries Puclications
114 Daisy Bank Road
Manchester M14 5QH, UK

Printed by Wright's (Sandbach) Limited
9 Old Middlewich Road
Sandbach, Cheshire CW11 1DP UK

Table of Contents

Acknowledgements

My deepest appreciation to: -

David and Sally Goudy for their proof reading of the manuscript and Sally's tireless efforts in making sure that my grammar was correct.

Also to David Goudy and Robert Williams for their more than generous comments in the foreword of this book.

Those very special people who encouraged me so much because they believed that I could and should write this book even when I didn't think I had the capability to do it.

Paul Hallam for his kind permission to use his photograph for the cover of this book.

Alex Robertson for all his expertise in preparing this manuscript for printing.

To my family for their support, in the highs and lows, the good times as well as the not so good, for their partnership in an amazing adventure.

Most important my deepest gratitude to my Jesus without whom none of this would have ever been possible.

FOREWORD 1

Someone has said, "Life is what happens while you are making other plans!"

Job, Joseph, Hezekiah and Paul had one thing in common. They discovered that bad things happen to good people. It rains on the just as well as the unjust. Of course, all of them overcame the vicissitudes of life and went on to gain great victories.

These 'leaves from a disciple's journal' is Gary Stevenson's own inimitable way of showing us that although we too face many a test in faith's examination, we also can graduate with honours.

Having known Gary for many years and having enjoyed his very gifted teaching ministry as one of our churches favourite speakers, I can recommend this very readable book to you. It is written in a humorous style that will have you smiling and nodding your head in agreement. You too will identify with God's guidance, interventions, and divine appointments in his stories of Christ's grace and provision.
Enjoy.

David Goudy
Pastor – Moira Pentecostal Church, Northern Ireland

FOREWORD II

The friendship of Gary and I goes back to the 1980's, when we met at Christian Conventions at that time. There was immediate identification with his sense of humour and enjoyment of fun, which is interwoven, throughout this very readable book. At the same time there was also the recognition of a deep love of The Lord and a wonderful knowledge of His Word.

Since then our local fellowship have gained immensely from his anointed and challenging ministry, having 'reminders' from a number of the incidents recorded in this book of those times together.

Behind the testimony and witness incorporated in these Chapters, is a close walk with his Lord, through some difficult and 'faith-sapping' experiences. Gary's ministry shall continue and further testimony will come forth, in preaching and writing, for the benefit of the Body as a whole. Go for it Gary!

"Just over the hill is a beautiful valley, but you must climb the hill to see it!"

Bob Williams
Pastor – Good News Fellowship, Yate, Bristol

Introduction

I suppose the reasons for writing this book is rather like the 'memorial stones' mentioned in Joshua Chapter 4 – that in the midst of the varied circumstances of life, the challenges and the trials, this book, like the 'stones' of Joshua, serves as a reminder of the grace, mercy, faithfulness and love of God showered upon a life and ministry.

This book is not an exhaustive chronological story of my life, rather a collection of incidents under different headings taken from a period of 23 years of full-time ministry around the globe. These are areas of our Christian life that are relevant to us all. So I trust that in some measure you will be encouraged, and even challenged by each of the different sections.

In the Old Testament there is a Prophet of God called Habakkuk, his name means to "embrace" but it can also be translated "wrestler" or even "struggler".

The book of Habakkuk reveals the prophet's struggle to "embrace" the ways of God in the situation in which he finds himself, and so he asks God questions, he wrestles and struggles with the age-old questions of "How long?" and "Why?".

In the mid seventies some friends and myself formed a Christian group, we toured around Northern Ireland singing at various church meetings and coffee bars. Here is a line from a song that we wrote in the midst of the bombs and bullets of war-torn Belfast.

"For we are reduced to fear the terror and the tears but what is that to prove? You can do your worst and I will still be free".

Although written at a particular time, in a particular situation, that line has come back to me many times in different countries and situations.

When there have been times of fear, when terror strikes your heart and tears begin to flow, no matter what is our lot in this life – WEEBLES RULE! (***Weebles wobble, but they don't fall down***).

Sorry, that's not very spiritual, is it? OK, here is a Scripture then.

2 Corinthians 4:8-9 (NIV)

We are hard pressed on every side, but not crushed; perplexed, but not in despair; persecuted, but not abandoned; struck down, but not destroyed.

"You can do your worst and I will still be free".

I would love you to read this book and find the answers to those questions in your life but alas in these pages you will not. There are, for all of us, times and seasons when we have far more questions than we do answers.

But my desire is that through these pages you will laugh, cry, be encouraged and understand that you are not the only one who wonders at times, "What is going on"? – and says to God, "It shouldn't happen to a Christian".

Names have been omitted or changed to protect the definitely guilty.

New Beginnings

"There has to be a beginning before there can be an end". Life is full of new beginnings, from the moment when our Mum took us to the classroom on our first ever day at school and left us there to face the great unknown – through to the time when we eventually left school and went out into the "big bad world" as it was known, starting our first job, seeking to embark on our chosen career – to the time when you gazed into his or her eyes and said "I do". What a new beginning that was! When you thought you knew all there was to know about marriage and very quickly learned that you knew absolutely nothing.

And of course, the greatest of all new beginnings, when under the conviction of the Holy Spirit you surrendered your life to Jesus Christ, which started an exciting journey of continual new beginnings, which for me up to the present moment has been 33 years.

Testimony

There is much that I could say with regard to my own personal testimony, of the process by which I came to bow the knee and accept Jesus as my Saviour and Lord. I am not going to do that. Sufficient to sum up my testimony in a phrase that I heard Mel Tari use in a Conference many years ago. "You can live in a cow shed but that doesn't make you a cow, you can smell like you have lived in a cow shed but that doesn't make you a cow, you can make the same noises as a cow but even that doesn't make you a cow. To be a cow you must be born into the family of a cow.

Well that's my testimony! I can't remember a time when I wasn't in church or involved in some aspect of church life. I was in all the right places, doing all the right things, making all the right noises, but I had never ever made a personal commitment to Jesus Christ, until February 1969, a matter of months before the troubles started in Northern Ireland.

God's servant

I worked in an engineering factory, and Friday was always the best day of the week, when you received your week's wages and had the weekend off. Along with some 250 other workers I headed out of the factory gates on my way home. As I made my way out, someone grabbed my arm, I turned around to see who was holding my arm. It was a small elderly man. He didn't work in the factory, I had never seen him before and I have never seen him since. He looked up at me and said, "You need to give your life to Jesus Christ", let go of my arm and disappeared into the crowd.

For the first time in my life, although not fully understanding it with my mind, I knew that what he had said was the answer. I am here today, because of the faithfulness of that little servant of God, and I will look forward to meeting with him.

I remember clearly after that encounter outside the factory saying to God that there were two things that I never wanted to do – "I never want to preach" and "I never want to travel" – **NEVER** say **NEVER**. So for 23 years those two things are the very things I have been doing on a full-time basis for the Lord. **Guess who won?** Now I have it worked out! On the basis of previous experience I have said to the Lord, "I NEVER want to go to Barbados".

Ministry?

As a member of a fellowship in Belfast I was particularly thrilled when after one evening meeting the Leadership approached me and asked me to fulfil a ministry for the fellowship. I thought to myself, "at last they have recognised my true potential", and anyway I could play the guitar better than the guy who was leading the praise and worship. So I waited with bated breath!

I suppose I should have heard the alarm bells when they added the words "we want you to do it faithfully", but I had said yes. And so this "*ministry*" was revealed with the words "we want you to put out the **chairs**".

CHAIRS – No! The word he used was ***ministry.*** Putting out chairs was a menial task, not a ministry. So how many know that I was thrilled to serve, and that I did it with joy? Well if the truth were told I hated it, and certainly initially did not do it with any semblance of joy, but I had said yes.

The problem was that to put out the chairs you had to go earlier than anyone else, and when the meeting was over, and everyone was off getting a burger, I was left to put the chairs away and tidy up after "mucky" Christians.

But the Lord had to deal with me over that, and I mean deal with me. The Lord viewed it as ministry to Himself, I certainly didn't, and we had a love hate relationship for a while – He loved me and I hated the work He had given me to do.

Until a revelation came, it may not be revelation to you, but it certainly was to me. I discovered that as I put out the chairs I could pray over every one! WOW – "Lord bless the person that will be sitting in this chair tonight" – "Lord you know the need of the person sitting in this chair, would you meet their need".

And what a joy it was, having fulfilled my ministry to sit back and see the Lord touch the lives of people and know that in some way I had a small part to play in their need being met.

So you see the reality is, there has to be a beginning before there can be an end. More often than not, particularly with the men and women of the Bible, we see as it were their "end" but many times fail to recognise their small "beginnings".

Test of faith

A matter of two months after that encounter outside the engineering factory in Belfast, a wonderful girl came into my life, my first real love. She had such a gentle spirit.

Suddenly my life had changed in a remarkable way. I found a faith that carried me through the bombs and the bullets of my beloved Province. I found a love that so enriched my life. And then in a moment, it seemed like it all fell apart with the dreaded word "**Cancer**".

"Why"? How could that happen? Surely this is not the way things are supposed to be?

And over the next six months, to watch the love, the treasure of your life, waste away before your eyes – when you cry and pray until the pain is so great you can no longer speak – and day in, day out, moment by moment, there is a cry (*or more like a scream*) in your heart.

18

It has been rightly said that when these things come across our paths they will either make us "**bitter**" or "**better**". I suppose I chose that by God's grace this horrible situation that had visited my life was somehow going to make me better.

And the hardest part of all, when you have to face the reality of releasing, letting go that wonderful gift back to God, who had "loaned" her to me for a brief moment of time, a short season, a gift who had added so much to my life.

Hurt, loss and pain can have, if we are not careful, a tremendously negative effect on our lives. Withdrawing into oneself, the fear of facing a repeat situation down the road, never making meaningful relationships for fear of losing the person and being hurt yet again.

But they often say that "time is a healer" and so some six years down the road and having met a beautiful girl from Southern Ireland, we were married in June 1976.

North meets South

How I met Dilys is rather an interesting and I believe a God-ordained, miraculous event.

A group of friends, mostly from Southern Ireland and a few of us from the North went on a camping holiday to Scotland, to Harris and Lewis. We had a wonderful time of fellowship and friendship, so much so that a reunion was arranged in Dublin, Southern Ireland.

Those of us from the North travelled down to join with our new-found friends. We were having a meal in the house of the lady that organised the trip, when Dilys walked in. She lived in the house, but had not been part of the trip, and she was introduced to those of us from the North.

That evening the whole party, including Dilys went for a walk along Dun Laoghaire pier outside Dublin. On the way back the group fragmented with different ones getting involved in conversations. I happened to find myself with Dilys and we began talking. I suppose for the first time I found that I was able to share from my heart, my hopes and dreams for the future and to find that many of those were the same for Dilys, particularly with the desire to serve God fully in whatever way that meant.

Confirmation

That was Saturday night then on Sunday morning, another girl from the holiday took me to a local House-Church. In the meeting that morning the sense of finding a soul-mate gripped me and I felt the Lord say to me that Dilys was to be my wife.

So I promptly said to the Lord, "You had better tell her, because I am not."

On driving back to the house for lunch, who did we see standing at the bus stop, having been to another meeting? It was Dilys, so we gave her a lift back to the house.

After lunch those of us that had travelled down from the North made the return journey home. That night at home in bed I couldn't sleep so I decided to write to the friend who organised the trip, and in the letter explain what I had felt about Dilys, and asked her if Dilys had mentioned anything at all to her about me?

On my way to the factory on Monday morning I posted the letter first class. Tuesday, Wednesday came and went, as did Thursday, this was most unusual because I was sure I would get a phone call from my friend as she was always very prompt and well-organised.

I arrived home from work on Friday, still no news. I couldn't take it any longer. So at about 6.30pm I phoned the house in Dublin. And lo and behold! Dilys answered the phone as everyone else was out, so in my awkwardness I blurted out that I would be down in the morning, something that was not at all pre-planned.

That night Dilys went to a prayer meeting and informed the others that I was coming down the following day. Their response was one of surprise as they said, "well normally he lets us know in advance".

Late night delivery!

Dilys and her housemates arrived back from the prayer meeting after 11 pm and as they opened the door, there was my letter on the mat. Why it had not arrived beforehand, who knows? And certainly it hadn't been there at 6.30pm when I had phoned, and there are no mail deliveries that late anyway, but the letter had arrived.

My friend made Dilys and herself a cup of coffee and proceeded to read the letter out loud in the presence of Dilys. Had I known that I certainly would not have made the journey the following morning.

Dilys and my friend stayed up for many hours talking and praying, and panic set in as at about 8am my car pulled up outside their front door.

Well the rest is history as they say, and so began an adventure that was to take us several times around the world, seeking to serve God together with all our hearts.

Again forgive me for omitting huge chunks of our lives. But after a series of miraculous events, believing that God had called us to work in full-time ministry in Israel, facing great opposition, not from outside the Body of Christ, but from within (*how strange! – unfortunately all too common*), we stepped out in faith with only two rucksacks and went to Jerusalem.

Death vs Destiny

Miracle boy

When my mum was 4 months pregnant with me she slipped on the rug and fell as she was getting out of bed. Two days later she began to bleed and was rushed into hospital for tests.

During those tests they were unable to find a heartbeat and for two days that remained the situation. On the third day my mum called in the nurse and said that she felt the baby move, which was greeted with scepticism by the nurses and doctors as they were convinced that the baby in her womb was dead.

But on my mum's insistence that she had felt the baby move, they proceeded to do the tests again, only to discover a faint heartbeat.

Although born three weeks early in the Jubilee Hospital in Belfast I am here to tell the tale. Any time the doctor saw me he would always say to my mum that I was a "miracle boy". I suppose in hindsight that in itself causes you to be aware that the hand of God was on your life, even before any of us were consciously aware of it.

Australia

At the age of nine we as a family decided to emigrate from Belfast to Adelaide, Australia, necessitating five weeks on a liner visiting different parts of the world, NO

SCHOOL – wonderful! I suppose that is why I have such an affinity with the place. We stayed the regulation two years before returning home.

The saying goes "boys will be boys", I suppose that's true to some extent. While in Australia with a friend of mine a bit of push and shove developed into a playful wrestling match, which somehow got to the place where I was on the ground with him on top of me with both his hands around my throat.

And suddenly what was a game became a frightening situation as I tried to struggle to break free only to find his hands tightening around my throat. I tried to shout, I could hear the words in my head but nothing would come out of my mouth.

I could feel myself losing consciousness, I don't know what happened, whether it was the fact that I was losing consciousness or the fact that my face was changing colour, but he let go, and I lay there for a while gasping for breath before fully coming around.

I don't relate this incident for any other reason than to say that even at a young age things like that can have a profound impact on your life and in some ways focus you as to what is important in this life.

Helpless spectators

Another incident happened, again in Australia many years later, as my wife, daughter and I were driving along a two-lane carriageway going to a meeting in the suburbs of Sydney. We were following a truck, which had three sheets of "plate" metal on the back, when the truck decided to shed its load. We were in a helpless and hopeless situation, mere spectators as this nightmare unfolded.

The first sheet of metal bounced on the road in front of us and went to our right. The second did the same and went to the left of us and the third sheet of metal hit the road in front of us and lay flat and we proceeded to drive over it.

On a wing and a prayer

We were flying from Jacksonville via Dallas and were now on the final leg of our USA tour on our way to Australia.

About 30 minutes out of Los Angeles the Captain came over the intercom and requested us not to be alarmed if we saw the emergency services coming out to meet the plane on landing, as this was purely a precautionary measure.

He went on to say that soon after take off from Dallas "one of our engines" had failed. He was so calm and reassuring, "one of our engines" – hey, what's one engine, after all we have several others, no problem.

The problem was that I was sitting level with the wing of the plane. Well I counted one engine on my side and I presumed there was one on the other side.

So then, now we have a bigger problem – "one of our engines has failed" – NO Mr. Captain – 50% of our engines have failed! We are flying on one engine!

Well I am here to tell the tale, so everything was fine and the emergency services did their job and all was well.

But I thought how the Captain had phrased it made all the difference – that is, if you were not sitting next to the wing.

A little aside: have you noticed when the Stewardesses go through their pre-flight safety instructions? Part of what they say is, "In the event of having to land on water, your life jacket is under your seat etc".

No one "lands" on water, you crash into water. I mean can you imagine the Captain saying, "I am fed up landing on the runway, I am going to land on water today"?

The fact of "landing" on water is so reassuring, isn't it – NOT!

Anyway, I am not saying that just because these things happened to me that it means that God's hand is on me and not on others, I do not mean in any way to imply that. But it is incidents such as these that make you more aware that there are plans for each of our lives that go beyond our understanding.

Death to Life

Over the years I have ended up preaching in many different and unusual situations from mansions to mud huts and everything in between. Certainly one of the most unusual places has to be a building in Yate, regularly used by a Fellowship, but during World Wars 1 & 2 it was used as a mortuary and a post-mortem room including a Chapel of Rest.

I find it ironic in a wonderful way that for some 30 years what was a place of literal death has now become a place of life and destiny.

Provision

Any step of faith, no matter what it is or where it is, will always be tested. One of the major areas of that testing is in the area of provision.

Philippians 4:19 (NKJV)

And my God shall supply all your need according to His riches in glory by Christ Jesus.

Now that is a wonderful Scriptural truth, but don't you just love it when God in His infinite wisdom leaves it to the last minute? Why does He do that? I mean if it was left up to us, we would certainly do it differently.

The unseen hand of God

We were in a prayer meeting in Bethlehem one Saturday morning, the following day our School fees for studying Hebrew were due, which caused us a little bit of a problem, as we didn't have any money to pay for the fees.

So as you can understand the topic of our prayers was for God somehow to supply this very urgent need. But God had initiated a series of events, which we at that time knew nothing about.

A friend of ours from Ireland was attending a Conference in America and while in one of the morning meetings, he felt God prompting him to send us some money. So he said to God, "If that is you, I want to meet someone today who knows Gary and Dilys and is going back to Jerusalem tomorrow".

Now if I had been there, my advice to him would have been "please don't make it so hard". The Bible talks about putting a fleece before God, well that's a whole flock of sheep for goodness sake.

Anyway, the afternoon came and went. Someone then invited him back to their chalet for coffee after the evening meeting. He knocked on the chalet door; When a girl opened it, he realised it was the wrong chalet, so he asked where this particular person was staying, and was given directions.

He was about to walk away when he stopped, turned round, and said, "Excuse me you don't happen to know Gary and Dilys Stevenson by any chance do you?" To which she replied, "Yes I do, they attend the same fellowship in Jerusalem."

Yes! you have guessed it, the next question was, "When are you going back to Jerusalem", to which she replied, "Tomorrow". "Hold on", he said, "I have something for you".

Bethlehem

That girl arrived in to Bethlehem at the end of the prayer meeting and handed us an envelope. Hurriedly we opened it to find more money than was needed for the fees, only to discover when we went the following day that they had put the fees up and it was exactly the right amount.

I want to say that even behind the scenes when we are not aware of it, God is working to meet the need that we have in our lives, as we seek to serve Him.

The reality of the faithfulness of God in provision is without question, but there is another side to the coin that I must mention.

There are some people who do not value the ministry at all, and still some who adopt an attitude of "You keep them humble God and we will keep them poor". People that associate the word "Christian" with the word "FREE".

On one occasion, I was speaking at a church near where I lived, which shall for obvious reasons remain nameless. At the end of the meeting the treasurer came to me and said, "You don't live far away do you?" I should have known then that something was amiss. The treasurer then proceeded to hand me to the exact one penny the price of a litre of fuel.

A 'token' gesture

On another occasion I had to drive several hours to do an all-day Sunday at this particular church. After the evening meeting I was handed a rather thick envelope, at which my heart understandably leapt with joy.

I arrived home in the early hours of Monday morning and sleepily crawled into bed; the following morning I opened this rather bulky envelope to see that it contained, not numerous twenty, ten or even five pound notes, but "*petrol tokens*".

My ministry gift was petrol tokens! That was a rather practical gift; We couldn't feed the family on them, but hey the car needs fuel, RIGHT. There was only one very slight problem with it though, they were only redeemable halfway down the M6 motorway, you had to spend as much getting there to put something in the tank.

While on a three month ministry trip in the U.S.A. we were booked to speak at what would have been considered a quite "*well-to-do*" church. At the end of the meeting, after some very kind comments from the Pastor with regard to our ministry, he announced that he was going to take up a special offering for us.

Of course you being spiritual wouldn't have been tempted to sneak a look as the offering baskets were brought to the platform! But I did! It looked rather a sizeable amount. But at the end of the service when the time came for us to leave, we received none of the special offering, but were presented with only the usual "honorarium".

It is just as well that ministry is a calling, for if it was a job, you would never in your wildest dreams do it, in fact if some people treated their local plumber or electrician the way they treat the ministry they would never get a job done.

Freely receive, freely give

We were invited to do a "camp-meeting" in Eastern U.S.A. My responsibility was the morning Bible Studies, as well as being part of the ministry team for the evening "celebrations".

On the second day of the Bible Studies a lady came to us and said that the Lord had prompted her to give us some money, then turned around and left, so that was fun, wasn't it?

Then in one of the evening celebrations there was a special offering that was going to overseas missions; I turned to Dilys and asked what she thought. Both of us, independently, had the same figure in mind, the problem being we actually had no money, so we agreed to put in an I.O.U.

We had a blessed week in the Bible Studies as well as the celebrations. On the last morning the same lady who had spoken to us several days before came to us and said,

"You remember that I told you that the Lord had prompted me to give you some money? Well He has changed it". I thought to myself, "Ah well, easy come easy go". She went on to say that the Lord had asked her to double the amount.

Well the new amount turned out to be the exact amount that we had pledged for missions, so we received it gratefully with one hand and willingly gave it with the other.

Later that day we were due to get the coach to the airport, we had just about enough money to cover the coach fare, but had no money for the actual flight ticket home. The Pastor who had organised the "camp meeting" informed us that a man, whom we shall call John, had offered to give us a lift.

First class

A couple of hours later John arrived, and as we were loading the bags into the car, the Pastor slipped an envelope into my pocket. So off we went, as we presumed to the coach terminal. John started to drive us not on the main roads into town but further into the country, until we arrived at a small airfield. John wasn't giving us a lift to the coach, but to his private plane, and promptly flew us to the International airport.

After getting to the departure terminal and saying our heartfelt thanks and goodbyes, I then opened the envelope that the Pastor had slipped into my pocket. Checking the amount in the envelope with the cost of the one-way tickets home – yes, you have realised it, the Lord had done it again, there was enough for the tickets and a good meal before the flight home.

Let me just mention this as I bring this chapter to a conclusion. In 23 years of full-time ministry we have only had one ticket pre-booked and pre-paid for by someone else. That was a flight from Switzerland to France for two weeks of meetings in Paris. We have been salaried for only one year of those 23, which was as Assistant Pastor of a church in Sydney, Australia.

I say that for no other reason than to give all the glory to God.

Bugs And All That

Isaiah 28:20 (NIV)
The bed is too short to stretch out on, the blanket too narrow to wrap around you.

How many know that if the bed you are trying to sleep in is too short for you or the covers are too narrow and keep falling off that there is no way in the whole world that you are ever going to get a good night's sleep or rest.

In over 23 years of full-time ministry and in particular travelling overseas, you end up staying and sleeping in all sorts of "wonderful" situations, and as if that was not challenging enough, eating all sorts of "wonderful" food.

Horror Hotel

On my first trip overseas to Africa I was travelling with a young man who we shall refer to as Philip. We had arrived in Lagos in the middle of the monsoon season and because we had missed our onward flight, we ended up insisting that the airline put us up at an hotel, rather than stay overnight in the airport lounge (*mistake One!*).

So they piled us into a mini-bus to take us to a hotel; Of course the mini-bus broke down, didn't it, just outside the airport, and some 45 minutes later we continued on our journey. We arrived at the Hotel and were taken to the restaurant for a meal, using stepping stones to avoid the pools of water; walking into the restaurant and stepping on the carpet the water started to bubble up through the carpet.

After a decidedly "average" but still welcome meal, we were informed that we were not staying at that hotel but were ferried to another one – this "new" hotel was so "new" it wasn't completed yet. Bare plaster, no electricity, but at least a bed of sorts. At this stage we were so shattered we just crawled into our beds only to find that the beds were already inhabited, by BUGS. By the morning we were black and blue where we had been on the menu for the hotel residents.

I don't know why I always ended up in places during the monsoon season, maybe God is trying to say something.

Beyond expectations

I was in the Philippines, on the Island of Panay, teaching in a Bible School. Part of the course for these wonderful young men and women was to have outreach meetings at night. On this occasion I was asked to go along with the students and to preach. So we all piled into a mini-bus (*of sorts*) and headed out to where the tarmac ended, to a community centre, which consisted simply of an open-air basketball court amidst some houses.

On the way the thunder and lightning started, rain coming down like "stair rods" (*that dates me a bit*), and of course in situations like that you think of all sorts of "spiritual thoughts" like, "Let's cancel and come back tomorrow".

Now outreaches in the Philippines consist of showing a film, a film by the way which has seen more repeats than any program on the television, and then someone preaching, ME.

I remember seeing the projectionist standing with an umbrella over him and the projector, and thinking, if lightning strikes, his eyes will light up.

Well eventually my turn came, and I marched out in the pouring rain, Bible in hand, to the only place where there was light, one hurricane lamp. Now, this is important; if you are ever in a situation where you are in darkness with only one light, never ever wear a white shirt. One lamp, plus a white shirt attracts everything and I mean everything.

Picture the scene, preaching in the pouring rain, rain dripping off your nose onto your Bible, everything with wings being attracted to you, eating you alive, some so big you could put saddles on them. Yet no one moving, hungry to hear God's Word, and the absolute joy of seeing people coming to Christ in conditions that maybe you and I would never continue in or expect anything to happen in.

I love the Philippines, I love the openness of the people, and I so love their sense of fun.

All the trimmings

Along with a group of people we had a Ministers Conference in San Fernando, before going in teams to various parts of the Philippines. With three others, I was appointed to go way up into the mountains to a Bible School, where we were involved in teaching during the day and a Conference at night.

On our arrival, after a journey of some 7 hours in less than ideal transport, we were shown to our "Spartan" accommodation. The sole source of light in the room consisted of a jam-jar filled with petrol with a wick through the top of the lid. My travelling companion refused each night to go into the room until it was lit – guess who had to light it? As both of us originally came from Northern Ireland it was rather a strange experience, as in our culture these are not 'lights' but 'petrol-bombs'.

We were informed in advance by one of our hosts that in the bathroom there was a spider, to which was added the phrase, "If you are going to kill it, make sure you do, as it will come after you". Comforting thought, needless to say I never showered with my back to the spider. The shower facilities by the way consisted of a large metal bowl, which you stood in, and a metal cup, with which you poured the cold water over yourself.

The following morning on going for a shower, we discovered that the large metal bowl had gone missing. We decided to go hunting for it after breakfast, I must admit we were not very happy to find it, as we discovered that they were using our "shower bowl" to mix the rice for lunch. It is amazing how "little" things like that can cause you to start fasting.

All shook up

There was also a couple there from Canada who were visiting some of their missionaries. The wife was a very sophisticated lady who had struggled with the very long, dusty journey up to the mountains.

This particular evening as we were sitting around eating our evening meal, she began to scream hysterically and slumped to the floor. As we rushed to her aid we discovered that a "flying cockroach" had flown straight into her ear. We had to hold her down as we removed the cockroach with tweezers.

Now if that wasn't enough for the poor lady, a number of days later, she was speaking in the morning meeting, when in the distance a sound like thunder could be heard, the problem being it was a bright, clear, sunny morning. As she continued into her message the noise got louder and louder, until the realisation that this "thunder" was in fact an earthquake.

The sense of powerlessness was overwhelming as we faced this power of nature, realising that whatever is going to happen is going to happen no matter what you do or do not do. I suppose it could be said that fortunately we were up in the mountains with not many buildings and not a large population, which limited the scale of damage.

After it was over, and the hours of aftershocks had subsided, in my nervousness I approached the lady, opened my mouth before putting my brain into gear and said, "Let me know where you are speaking next, so I can make sure not to be there".

I am not sure after those experiences whether or not she has ventured on another overseas journey.

Varied diet

I suppose that when it comes to food the more that you travel the greater the opportunity is of eating all sorts of weird and wonderful things.

One of my earliest experiences was fish-heads floating in palm-oil stew. I don't know what happened to the rest of the fish, but it was just the heads, including the eyes, which also had to be eaten. Now, this palm-oil stew was a reddish colour, so the picture was more like fish-heads floating in "blood".

Along with this was a dish called "gari", a dish with the consistency of cement, this was rolled with the fingers into a ball, dipped into the palm-oil stew, and swallowed not chewed. The thing that I noticed quite quickly was that after dipping the "gari" into the stew, it stained your fingers, so who knows what it did to your insides.

I have eaten chicken's feet, shark, fish eyes, snake, and a number of dishes that looked to be very suspicious, but again one of the lessons I learned very early on in my travels, is that you don't say things like, "that was nice, what was it?" It is better not to ask.

Unfortunately there are times when you don't ask, but are still told.

Honoured guest

One of those occasions was again in the Philippines, when after a particular meal, which was supposed to be for us as "honoured" guests from overseas, the statement was made, "was that the first time you have eaten dog"? To which I replied with rather a strangled "yes".

Dog apparently is very expensive, and is reserved for special occasions and special guests. I want to say I am not that special, and no one should feel that they have to go out of their way just for me.

I was invited to do a Bible Study in one of the "stilt houses" in the Philippines. The Filipino people are so gracious and treat guests with tremendous honour, something we all could learn from. The lady of the house had gone out of her way to make some home-made ice cream for her "distinguished" guests.

Well, I have never seen ice cream like that or tasted ice cream like that in my life, but I ate it not wishing to offend. On finishing it (*I think I was last*) I set the plastic container to one side. We then continued in the study of God's Word and in ministry afterwards.

At the close of our time together the lady of the house was collecting the ice cream containers, I reached back to get mine, only to discover that an army of ants were crawling all over it, cleaning up what I had left. I grabbed it between my finger and thumb and handed it to her.

She took the container and simply blew all the ants off it. Then taking what I can only describe as a "dirty rag" masquerading as a handkerchief, she "spat", yes I did say "SPAT" into the container and wiped it with this rag, before placing the container back on the shelf for the next time.

So the immediate thought that sprang to my mind was, "She has done the 'washing up' like this several times before". Which wasn't really a thrilling thought to have at that moment.

Nepal

I had a friend who was in the diplomatic service based in Nepal, and of course because of his position was often invited to official banquets. On one particular occasion as guest of honour, a live monkey was brought in and ritually killed in front of the "honoured" guests. Then it was decapitated, and the crown removed, placed on a silver salver and passed around the assembled gentry, who each had to take a piece of the brain and eat it.

I asked our friend what he did, to which he replied that he took the smallest piece possible, excused himself, went on to the balcony and threw up.

Now in this last incident of this section, I want you, as you read it, to realise that my life as I knew it is over! That is if my daughter can a) catch me or b) find me.

Travelling is portrayed as attractive but believe me it is not all that glamorous, particularly if you happen to be travelling with a young child. On one occasion we flew from London, Heathrow to Shannon, Ireland and from there to New York. We checked our bags in for the onward flight to Washington DC, only for the announcement to come through that the flight had been delayed. Of course as you can imagine we were all totally shattered at this stage, wondering what planet we were on never mind which country we were in.

Lost control

Consequently the announcement of a delay was relayed on several more occasions. It was a nine-hour delay at this stage; I had my daughter on my knee as we drifted in and out of consciousness.

Suddenly in the midst of my sleep I felt a warm liquid running down my leg, my first thought was "I haven't"? I honestly thought that as I was so tired that I had completely lost control of my bodily functions.

In fact it was my daughter, whatever way she was lying on my knee her nappy (*diaper*) failed to come into play and I was left wet and embarrassed, as our bags had been checked through earlier and I had no means of changing my trousers. When the time came to board the onward flight, it must have been quite a sight to see me trying to skulk on to the plane, holding whatever I could in front of me to maintain my dignity.

Divine Encounters

There are times in all of our lives when we need God to break through, and it is in times like those that often we see the supernatural hand of God move, or He brings people across our path at those specific moments.

I remember a particular period of time not long after we went as missionaries to Israel, which was a real, for want of a better phrase, "crisis of faith". We had a house full of overseas visitors, and limited transport. Hence I had to leave earlier than everyone else, to get the bus to the prayer meeting that started at 8 a.m., of course as you can imagine, that thrilled me even more.

So I walked down to the bus-stop, I suppose with the weight of the world on my shoulders, wondering whether or not we had made the right choice in giving up everything and coming to the mission field. I stood there on that empty street, waiting for the bus, praying, tossing everything over in my mind.

I looked up the road to see if the bus was coming, but when I turned back there was a man standing there. I hadn't seen him coming, and there is no way in the world he could have arrived there without me spotting him. He was dressed in usual Arab clothing, but his eyes and his smile absolutely transfixed me. He didn't say a word, but I was so aware of all the things that had consumed my mind just melting away, like a great weight being lifted off me.

47

I turned away to see the bus coming in the distance, but on turning back the man had gone. I looked around to see if I could see where he went, but nothing, and there was no way that he could have gone anywhere in that brief moment.

But all I know is that when I boarded that bus and arrived at the prayer meeting, I was in such a place of peace, a place of assurance that God had it all under control.

Milan, Italy

We were on a lengthy ministry trip through Europe. One of those places on our itinerary was Milan, Italy. The problem was, the only contact we had in Milan was a phone number.

On arrival in Milan we phoned the number and subsequently were collected at the airport by the Pastor. We were informed that we were most welcome to stay for a few days but as regarding ministry there was nothing really available.

He invited us to travel with him to Lake Como where he was speaking at one of their branch churches. During the course of the second meeting he invited me to share a little bit of testimony about our time in Israel, which I was most grateful to do.

That night after the meeting over supper he asked me, totally out of the blue, if I could minister the Word the next day. We had a blessed time in the meeting and the Lord graciously used us in both the Word of Knowledge and in Prophecy.

On the way back to Milan this dear brother asked us to speak at the main church on Sunday morning. At the end of the service that morning the Lord gave me a Prophetic Word for both the Pastor and for the church.

As it happened the Pastor himself was my interpreter that morning, and as I began to prophesy concerning him, the tears began to flow, and through the tears he related to the congregation what the Lord was saying concerning his life and ministry and then also the church. Pretty soon the whole church was in tears as the Word of the Lord encouraged their hearts.

At the end of the service, there was an animated discussion going on between the Pastor and the congregation. The Pastor then turned to us and said, "We as a church would love you to stay for two weeks to minister the Word into our lives".

We had such a blessed time in that place, not just in ministry but in love and fellowship as these dear folks took us not only into their homes but also into their hearts. I thank God for Divine Encounters. Even when in the natural you wonder how things could ever work out or fit into place, the Lord has it all in hand.

Many pieces, one picture

Can I say at this point, that for many of you reading this book, as you look at your lives it seems like all you have is a few pieces of the jigsaw. Yet they look so different and you wonder how on earth they fit into the "picture" of your life.

The temptation is to try and force things, but that's not the way. So can I say to you that even though those various pieces look like they could never fit together, in the plan of God for your life they DO fit, and He will unfold that "picture" of your life, as you look to and rest in Him. The assurance that we have is, what God starts He always finishes.

Crazy Itinerary

While planning a prospective ministry trip to Southern Ireland we felt a very strong sense that we should leave on the fortieth day. A close friend of ours very graciously offered to arrange our itinerary for us.

On our arrival in Dublin we discovered that there was no 'rhyme or reason' to this itinerary! Our first meeting was in Dublin, the next night down in Limerick 123 kilometres away, then back to Dublin, then west to Galway a further 136 kilometres, and so it continued night after night.

We had such a blessed time of fellowship in every place we went and the goodness of God was evident in every meeting as He spoke and ministered into people's lives.

On night number 39, we were due to speak at a meeting in a place called Carlow. I rang to confirm the time of the meeting and was regretfully informed that the meeting had to be cancelled. As I enquired further, I discovered that from our very first meeting in Dublin certain leaders, that were opposed to anything remotely to do with the things of the Holy Spirit, had been trying to trace where our next meeting would be, but had been unable to, because of the crazy itinerary (*the wisdom of God*).

They had finally caught up with us after a process of elimination on meeting number 39. The next morning, day 40 we flew out of Dublin having yet again experienced the faithfulness of God at work.

Twoomba, Australia

In the early hours of one morning whilst in Israel, my wife told me that I sat bolt upright in bed, eyes wide open, though still asleep, and said, "Twoomba, Twoomba", closed my eyes, and lay down again.

Apart from the obvious thought, that finally I had "flipped", my wife suggested that I look up an Atlas, to see if that name existed anywhere (*That's wisdom*).

Sure enough I discovered that indeed it was a place, it was a town in Queensland, Australia. For the next few days I spent time waiting on God with regard to "Twoomba", although we had never previously ministered in Australia, I felt the Lord reveal some specific Scriptures to me.

Some 4 years later we were invited to do some meetings in New South Wales, Australia. Whilst there we decided to try and contact a lady that we met in Israel some years before. We eventually got a contact number for her in Brisbane, Queensland. She in turn invited us up for a visit.

On our arrival she said, "I hope you don't mind but I have arranged three days of meetings for you in a place (*yes you guessed it*) called Twoomba".

It would not be prudent to go into details, but sufficient to say that the church had been through some massive difficulties, and the Word that I felt the Lord say to me some four years before, was absolutely relevant and hit the mark with tremendous impact.

I have had the privilege of seeing many things over the years, but the impact of the Word of God, not only preached but in the prophetic realm, I have rarely seen to that same extent.

Yad Vashem

This next encounter is rather an extraordinary one, and some may well question as to why it is in this section of the book. Yet, this encounter had such a profound effect on those of us who were involved, concerning the reality of the world we live in. You see, sometimes as Christians we can allow ourselves to get cosseted in some 'spiritual vacuum' and fail to see the real situations of life that people have and are living through and in.

During our time in Israel, part of what we did was to show tourists whose first trip to Israel it was around Jerusalem and other parts of the country.

One of the places we always took visitors was Yad Vashem, the Holocaust Museum in Jerusalem, we felt it was essential that people saw and in some measure experienced what man can do to his fellow man.

One of the most poignant moments happened to a friend of ours who was taking some people around the museum.

While showing them some of the horrific memorabilia he heard a lady screaming hysterically. He rushed over to where she was and tried in some measure to console and comfort her.

After a lengthy period of time she was a little calmer and in some measure able to talk, he discovered that her mother had been taken to one of the concentration camps, and she had never known specifically what had happened to her.

But on the wall of the museum was a picture of a German soldier standing behind a lady over an open grave, holding a rifle to her head, and yes you have realised it – that was her mother.

Reality hits home

It is a strange feeling being in Israel, you can be standing on a crowded bus, going to do normal everyday things and next to you a person holding on to the bar of the bus. Then you notice a number tattooed on their arm, and you suddenly realise that here, rubbing shoulders with you, is a survivor of the Holocaust.

And to them will I give in my house and within my walls a memorial ... an everlasting name [a "yad vashem"], *that shall not be cut off.* (Isaiah 56:5)

Miracles or What?

Some of the most striking things when you first start to read the New Testament are the miracles of Jesus. And then you discover the Words of Jesus when He says: -

John 14:12 (NKJV)

*Most assuredly, I say to you, he who believes in Me, the works that I do he will do also; and **greater works** than these he will do, because I go to My Father.*

So full of faith (or something) you are ready to face and take on any situation which presents itself.

Well, the first two people I ever prayed with both died! I mean how could that be? I read all the right Scriptures, prayed the right prayers, but they died. I was absolutely devastated. I had visions of me walking down the street and everyone moving across to the other side. "Don't let Gary pray with you" I am sure they would say, "unless you want to go to heaven".

And so in my devastation I said to the Lord, "I am never going to pray with anyone ever again", and I meant it.

Running scared

So over the next number of months I became very good at spotting people who needed prayer and avoiding them. But you know God will not let you do that for long. I was at this particular meeting in Dublin and at the end was talking to some of the leaders at the front of the church, and then I spotted her! And what was worse she had spotted me. There was a problem, there was only one door that served as both entrance and exit, and so God had me trapped!

And she started to move through the crowd towards me. You know when a disaster is about to happen, everything goes in slow motion, well it was like that, it took her "three weeks" to get to me.

Eventually she stood in front of me, and said the words I never ever wanted to hear again, "Brother Gary, would you pray for me". Well, it was there just around my Adam's apple, the word NO, but I could not get it out. I am sure she wondered what was wrong, but could I get that silly word out of my mouth?

Restored

So how many know that I didn't pray with a great deal of faith? I prayed the shortest prayer I could pray, so I could get out of there. This woman had a particularly obvious problem, so I prayed "God heal her, in Jesus Name". Well blow me, if God didn't do it!

I know it did a lot for that lady but it did more for me, in restoring me to a place where God could do in and through me what He wanted to do without me putting any limits on Him at all.

Can I leave you with this statement, "Don't allow past failures to hinder you today." God has got more for you than you can even imagine.

One of the strangest areas I have been involved in over the years has been in praying for women who medically could not conceive. Of course there are certain parts of the world where if a woman cannot conceive she is treated as a "second class" citizen and her husband can in turn take another wife.

One particular incident springs to mind out of the many. When in Ghana I prayed for a lady who found herself in this predicament. A number of months later I received a letter rejoicing in the fact that she was expecting her "miracle" child, but at the bottom of the letter was this phrase "*and it's all thanks to you*". I showed my wife the letter, rejoiced in the miracle and *destroyed* the letter!

Dream fulfilled

Joel 2:28 (NKJV)

And it shall come to pass afterward that I will pour out My Spirit on all flesh; Your sons and your daughters shall prophesy, **Your old men shall dream dreams, Your young men shall see visions**.

I want to say from the outset that I have more visions and very few dreams, for obvious reasons!

One particular night I had a dream concerning a very close friend of mine and a certain aspect of his business, then the dream suddenly switched and I saw a lady from his church walking down the street, heavily pregnant. This lady and her husband were considering adopting because she had failed to conceive although medically they could find no reason. But they were told that they were too old to adopt. They had gone through the whole traumatic IVF treatment in July 1998 but without success, which had devastated them.

The following day I phoned my friend and shared the dream that I had experienced. He asked me could he share it with the couple, to which I replied, if he felt that it would encourage their faith then please do. That was in September

1998. In November of that year I received a phone call to say that the couple were expecting a baby.

In the June of 1999 during my usual trip to Northern Ireland I had the wonderful joy of seeing the dream come to pass, and subsequently on July 23rd a beautiful baby boy, Adam, was born to this precious couple. At this moment in time, as I write (*December 2001*) they are expecting their second child.

I want to say that God is interested in, and cares about, every aspect of our lives.

Sight restored?

I had been away ministering in the South of England for the weekend and had decided to travel back late on the Sunday night rather than get caught up in the traffic the following morning.

I arrived home in the early hours of Monday morning absolutely shattered, and crawled into bed. I awoke a few hours later as the children had to get ready for school and to my total surprise I could see clearly (*I have been short-sighted most of my life*). I said to my wife that I had been healed and could see clearly without problem.

Then in a moment revelation came and reality dawned on me. In my exhaustion I had crawled into bed and had *forgotten* to take my contact lenses out – at least for a brief moment hope sprang eternal!

One of the strangest miracles that I have had the privilege to see was in the Philippines. At the end of one of the celebration meetings, as is usual in those parts of the world, hundreds of people came forward for prayer.

I went to this one lady who had brought her friend for prayer, to find that her friend was both deaf and dumb. The request for prayer was not as one would have presumed, for healing and release, but for Baptism in the Spirit.

I must admit to have been taken aback somewhat by this. As I continued in prayer, I was absolutely astounded, so much so I had to open my eyes to confirm what my ears were hearing.

This lady, who was deaf and dumb, was speaking so beautifully and clearly in her heavenly language. There is no way in the world she could speak naturally, and I suppose a part of you thinks "I wish she would have received her hearing and speech".

But to hear her speak in other tongues, as the Holy Spirit made it possible, for anything else was a complete impossibility, and to see the glow of joy on her face, is something I will never ever forget.

Speaking in Tongues

Let me mention a few things with regard to the rather controversial subject of "Speaking in other Tongues". These incidents were with regard to people who had difficulty with the validity of "Speaking in Tongues".

There was a Latin scholar who had tremendous problems in this area. This gentleman took ancient Latin manuscripts and translated them into English. He had come along to the meeting rather sceptical and just "happened" to be sitting behind my wife, who during the course of the meeting was quietly praying in tongues. To his absolute amazement he understood every word that she was saying, and was able to translate her praise and adoration to God. Totally convinced, subsequently he received the Baptism in the Holy Spirit and he too was "Speaking in other Tongues".

We had prayed for a Jewish lady in Israel, again who was unsure, but had come forward for prayer. As we prayed with her she began to pray in tongues. The wonderful thing was that my wife was able to tell her what she was praying, as she was speaking fluent Gaelic.

The opposite happened in Dublin when we prayed for a person who again began to pray in tongues. The amazing factor here was that this person spoke a phrase, as far as they were concerned, in "tongues", then they would say a phrase in English, which we recognised was in fact a direct translation – the reason being they were speaking in Hebrew, which we were able to understand because of our two years in Israel.

In His way

One problem is that many times when you are "on the road" you minister in one place, then the next night you are somewhere else. So apart from the times when obvious things take place in a meeting, you often don't hear of the ongoing testimonies of the people you have ministered to.

We were ministering in Dublin, Southern Ireland for one night before going on somewhere else, and I remember one particular lady had a rather unsightly lump behind her ear for which she came forward for prayer. Nothing obvious seemed to take place, and after the meeting we moved on to our next destination.

When we were in the same meeting almost exactly a year later, this same woman came to us and reminded us of the fact that we had prayed for her a year ago, and added the words "and nothing happened". I thought to myself "Thanks for reminding me". But she went on to say that she went home after the meeting, and was getting ready for bed, washing her face in the bathroom, when the lump came off in her hand.

Boy, you could make a fortune manufacturing that soap all right. The Lord is faithful to His Word, but I tell you what, He does it His way.

Take up the towel

In 1977 we assisted a friend of ours leading a tour group to Israel. This rather unusual incident took place up in Galilee.

Some of us had neglected to wear the regulation clothing and so were unable to go into one of the sites. We sat on the Mount of Beatitudes and spent some time in prayer whilst waiting for the others. During that prayer time we felt the Lord speaking to us that we should wash the feet of the others in the tour group.

Of course, when you receive something like that you immediately 'spiritualise' it. Well I mean God doesn't 'actually' want us to wash their feet but to be more caring towards them in a 'servant' type manner. But no matter how much we tried we could not get away from what we felt God had said.

Two nights later we had been given the use of a small building by the Sea of Galilee for our nightly prayer meeting. Some of the tour party had brought some towels along so that they could go swimming in the Sea of Galilee afterwards – strange!

Someone had gone to the back room of the hall to get a glass of water and came back and informed us that there were two basins on the floor below a water tap! Well that was it; we couldn't ignore it any longer. We informed our friend Mike, who graciously gave us the freedom to do what we felt in God to do, and while we prepared the necessary items he explained to the people what was to take place.

What a wonderful time of blessing seeing people set free as we moved in obedience to the Lord, some received a healing touch during the act of foot washing. A couple from Jerusalem were there, who later became very close friends, and the Spirit of Prophecy came upon them and they began to declare God's Word of encouragement over peoples lives.

One unfortunate aside to this remarkable incident: a gentleman from the South of England stood up as we began to wash the feet of the people and declared, "No one is going to wash my feet", and he promptly left and about half a dozen others went with him.

The day before we left Tiberias for the airport he picked up a nasty foot infection and was unable to leave with us and had to remain behind until his foot had recovered sufficiently to travel.

"We need a miracle!"

One of the duties I was assigned while in Israel was the "airport run". If anyone needed to be collected from or taken to Tel-Aviv airport, then that was one of my responsibilities.

This particular evening a couple were arriving in Israel and my wife and I had to collect them from Ben Gurion airport. We had a "communal" car, and on getting ready to leave for the airport had great difficulty getting it started. The reason could have been that the needle and the red light flashing indicated that we were out of fuel.

I asked my wife to go back into the house and see if anyone had any money for petrol. She eventually came out having asked the others and searched the house, with a definite "no money".

After several "prayerful" attempts we managed to get the car started. As you can imagine, not a lot of conversation went on in the car to the airport, but a lot of fervent, silent prayer and perspiration.

We somehow, eventually made it to the airport. On collecting our newly arrived guests, our primary thought was "God you need to help us get home".

With the bags loaded and the passengers safely seated in the back, I put the key in the ignition, and when much to my surprise it started first time, we made our way out of the airport complex towards Jerusalem.

As we were driving along, praying whilst trying to answer the million and one questions our visitors had, I glanced at the petrol gauge, only to notice that it had moved to a quarter tank.

Gauge stuck, the petrol was there all along? Maybe! But all I know is that not only did we do the 102-kilometre round trip, but also we spent the next two weeks driving on that quarter tank – and that, in Jerusalem and its suburbs, is an impossibility.

Deb's tale

One hot summer my youngest girl and young son were playing ball in the garden, and as always happens, the ball ended up going over the fence into the next door neighbour's garden.

They both went next door to ask for the ball back. The neighbours had a rather large young dog who for whatever reason decided it was going to jump up on my daughter and unfortunately snapped at her face. Of course you can imagine the pandemonium as they came running back to us screaming, my daughter's hand over her nose with blood going everywhere. We rushed her to the hospital to discover that the dog had bitten her nose.

The hospital examined her and decided she needed to go to the children's hospital in Manchester, and took us there by ambulance. My son wanted to come with us; in fact he refused to leave my daughter's side, such was his concern for his sister — while my daughter was more concerned with insisting that the neighbour's dog should not be put down.

After a rather lengthy in-depth examination at the hospital in Manchester it was decided to prepare her for plastic surgery. So we waited for the plastic surgeon to arrive and perform the operation. The dog had bitten right through to the cartilage in her nose and removed the skin.

On the surgeon's arrival he decided, after more extensive examination, to leave the surgery for a week, assuring us that waiting would not in any way hinder the success of the surgery.

We returned the following week, but after yet another lengthy examination, and much to our surprise and delight, the surgeon said that some skin had begun to form again over the cartilage — not enough to be seen with the naked eye, but sufficient for him to again defer the operation.

Over the next few weeks the skin began to grow back in a wonderful miraculous way and today, well, you would be hard pushed to see the scar on Deb's nose, and only then if you were specifically looking for it.

Sometimes we use the phrase "God is good" so glibly but I want to say as far as I am concerned "He is so very good."

Miracles Part 2 – Curacao

In 1982 I really felt the leading of the Lord to go to the island of Curacao in the Dutch Antilles, off the coast of Venezuela. I had no contacts there or anything arranged, but clearly felt the prompting of the Lord, and so I had planned to stay for a week.

This was around the time that they changed the currency in Israel back to the shekel from the Israeli lira. A friend of ours had managed to get me three shekels, which I had made up into key rings to take with me.

So all the arrangements were made to fly from Jacksonville via Miami to Curacao. We had been spending a few months ministering in the States.

Everything was ready and a friend was taking me to the airport. Unfortunately the friend happened to be late, and as you can imagine I was in a place of perfect peace! Well, it began with the letter "P" but it wasn't peace it was "panic".

Eventually they arrived and I threw my bags quickly into the car. My wife and our daughter were going to stay in the States so as I was about to get into the car she asked me to leave her some money. In my haste I reached into my back pocket and handed it to her.

Now this friend, bless them, who was late arriving, insisted on sticking to the speed limit the whole way to the airport, which as you can imagine blessed me even more. Of course we were late, so on arriving at the set-down point I said my goodbyes, grabbed my bags and ran into the departures lounge.

I handed my ticket to the gentleman at the check-in only to hear the words "I am sorry Mr. Stevenson you have missed the flight".

I asked about the next flight, which I was informed was in an hour's time. But he quickly added that I could not get on the next flight with my ticket as it was for the flight that I had missed and was not transferable. He said there were seats available and I could purchase a ticket from the ticket desk.

"I will make a way"

I reached into my pocket only to discover that in my haste on leaving I had handed my wife everything, money, credit cards, the lot. But as I walked away from the check-in I really felt the Lord impress in my heart the phrase "I will make a way where there is no way".

I went and sat down. When the time came for the next flight I went to the check-in desk and handed the man my "old" ticket. He looked at me as if I was "familiar", looked at the ticket, and said, "I am sorry Mr. Stevenson you cannot use this ticket on this flight, it was for the previous flight". He went on to say that there were seats available and I could purchase a ticket from the ticket desk. I thought to myself "that's what you think".

Again as I went to sit down, the phrase, "I will make a way where there is no way", kept burning in my heart.

Eventually the time came for the next flight, I marched up to the check-in and presented the man with the same ticket. His immediate response, as he looked at the ticket was, "You have been here before haven't you", to which I replied "Yes".

Now you know how when people think that you are not getting the message, they slow their speech down and accentuate their words.

"THIS ticket was for TWO flights ago, it is not transferable, YOU missed that flight, is that RIGHT". I said, "Yes". "You CANNOT use THIS ticket on THIS flight". I couldn't understand why his tone had changed.

He must have thought that the message was still not getting through, so he said, "Come here", and swung the monitor around, punched a few keys and said "This is the list for TWO flights ago, and there is YOUR name on the list". "YOU MISSED that flight". "Now here is the list for this flight ... And there ... is your name on the list". To which I replied "I will have non-smoking please".

Gift from Jerusalem

After booking into a hotel I spent the next two days looking around and familiarising myself with my new surroundings. I came across a rather beautiful and ornate synagogue.

I went inside and began to look around a museum that they had there. This was the oldest synagogue in the Americas, dating from 1732, this was their 250th anniversary celebrations. I began to talk to a man who I quickly realised was the Rabbi. I rather boldly asked if it was possible to have a meeting with him the following day as I had something to give him.

67

The following day armed with the three "Shekel" key rings I went to see the Rabbi. I presented him with one, and one to the synagogue on their anniversary, both were graciously accepted.

It was an amazing feeling among all the memorabilia in the synagogue museum to see this "Shekel" key ring occupy a prominent place.

As I was about to leave, a father and son came to see the Rabbi to finalise the arrangements for the son's Bar-Mitzvah, I asked the Rabbi if he would give the son the final "Shekel" key ring to honour his Bar-Mitzvah.

Surprise invitation

Again this was graciously accepted and I was issued with a surprising invitation to the Bar-Mitzvah celebrations, as one of the guests of honour, at the Hilton Hotel.

What a miracle it was as I sat at the top table that night in-between the President of the Synagogue and his wife, surprisingly watching a belly-dancer who had been flown all the way from Egypt for the celebrations.

During the course of the evening the wife of the President turned to me and said, "What religious group are you attached to?" To which I replied "Pentecostal". "Oh" she said "they are the ones that speak in tongues, I am really interested in that, tell me all about it please". The rest of the evening was spent in an in-depth discussion with this knowledgeable lady about Christianity.

Well certainly God was doing something unusual on this rather "bizarre" trip to Curacao, but it wasn't over yet.

On the Sunday morning after attending fellowship at one of the local churches I was walking back to where I was staying. I passed by a little church that had large iron gates, which were padlocked. There was something about this place that I couldn't put into words, yet I felt drawn to it.

I decided that I would walk round there in the evening to see if there was any sign of life.

You are late!

I walked around to the church about 7.15pm figuring that if any meeting was on it would start about 7.30pm, as things tended to start later than usual in that part of the world.

As I rounded the corner I noticed the gates open and a light on, and as I approached the entrance I noticed a lady and two men standing there. The lady greeted me with the words "You are preaching for us tonight aren't you?"

Apparently the Lord had spoken to them that morning saying that He was sending someone from overseas to minister the Word. The meeting actually was supposed to start at 7pm and so I was running a little late.

The Pastor and his wife were celebrating 50 years of overseas missions work that month and he had just recently gone blind.

I spoke that night as I felt the Lord was leading me from the Scripture "Whom shall I fear", and the Lord graciously gave me a Prophetic Word for the church. The Pastor, his wife and most of the congregation were in tears. They explained later something of the background of their lives and the present situation and said that I would have had to have lived there for the last 50 years to say some of the things I had said.

Such a wonderfully precious couple, who had faithfully served the Lord through all sorts of situations and challenges for so many years.

So that was Curacao, a remarkable trip, I certainly wouldn't have planned it that way, yet I wouldn't have changed anything at all.

You know what I have discovered over the years? Everybody wants a miracle, but nobody wants to be in the place where he or she needs one.

Valley of Achor

We often talk about and hear messages on the "mountain-top" and "valley experiences". Given a choice of course we all know which we would choose. But unfortunately the choice is not ours.

Hosea 2:14-15 (NKJV)

Therefore, behold, I will allure her, I will bring her into the wilderness. I will give her her vineyards from there, And the Valley of Achor as a door of hope; She shall sing there, As in the days of her youth, As in the day when she came up from the land of Egypt.

This is a strange statement, the Lord says "I will allure (*entice, flatter or persuade*) her", and look where He brings her, into the wilderness. As I said not the place of our choosing, but sometimes that is exactly what happens.

The word Achor is better translated as the valley of "trouble". So it says very clearly that even the valley of trouble can become for us a door of hope, and lead to a place of fruitfulness.

In truth of course the place where the reality of our faith is tested is not on the "mountain-top", when all is well thank you very much, but in the "valley" experiences of life.

Sometimes we just never use the brain that God has given us, and when you are seeking to serve God and passionate about the call of God you can get to the stage where you almost feel you are indestructible.

One of those occasions was some 12 years ago. Previous to this event a very dear and much respected Brother in the Lord had said to me "Gary, take the opportunities that God gives you to rest, to do just that".

Eight long months

I had just finished a series of 21 meetings in 14 days when the following morning I awoke to find that I had no voice at all, nothing, not even a whisper and for two weeks it stayed that way. The problem being, that after those two weeks the best that I could manage was a rather pathetic whisper, not the kind of thing that a preacher needs in his life.

I was referred to a specialist and subsequently had an exploratory operation to discover that I had damaged the vocal chords, and the cure? A word we all love to hear – REST. There was a little aside to this, the fact that there were no guarantees that my voice would return to any degree of strength to enable me to continue what I knew was the call of God.

For a very long 8 months that is the way it remained. When there are no guarantees I can tell you that you do a lot of heart-searching and suddenly your perspective on life and ministry changes dramatically.

I don't in any way want to over-dramatise it, but the only portion in Scripture that I can liken it to, is the incident in Genesis Chapter 22 concerning Abraham and Isaac, the sense of being willing to lay down the very thing that was a Gift of God.

That of course did not come easy. It was a process that took time, but to arrive at the place where you realise that though circumstances may change, though for whatever reason you may not be able to fulfil the very ministry you believe God had called you to do, nothing can change relationship. Our relationship with the Lord is not, or should not be, based on what we can or cannot do.

After 8 months when my voice returned to the extent that I could begin to preach again, the only way I can describe how I felt is, that I value the privilege of ministry much more than I ever did, but I hold it much more lightly.

Letter from Oz

Having spent two very blessed and happy periods of ministry in Australia, we returned to England because of impending family matters.

Not long after our arrival back in England I received a derogatory letter from a Church leader in Australia, who was greatly upset because we had left earlier than our stipulated agreement.

Of course when you receive a letter such as that there is something that rises up within you to respond in kind.

Some would claim it to be "righteous anger" but that is only an excuse to justify getting even with someone who has deeply wounded you. I do wish that some Scriptures were not in the Bible.

Matthew 5:23-24 (NKJV)

Therefore if you bring your gift to the altar, and there remember that your brother has something against you, leave your gift there before the altar, and go your way. First be reconciled to your brother, and then come and offer your gift.

That is the Scripture that I was challenged with. I knew that I had nothing against him, but it says if *he* has something against *me*, that I had to make the first move in reconciliation, now that's unfair. So yes, I had to write a letter but not the letter I wanted to write.

It took a long time and many failed attempts to write the kind of letter I needed to write, and tears were shed. As far as I knew as I searched my own heart I had done nothing to offend this brother, nothing to necessitate this attack on me.

But eventually I wrote the letter, It went something like this – "My dear Brother if I have ever done anything to offend you or hurt you in any way then please forgive me".

I must say writing that letter did more for me than possibly it would do for him, but then that is the purpose of Matthew 5:23-24. There was a tremendous sense of release when I actually posted the letter, a freedom that came to my own heart. I heard nothing back until almost exactly two years later a letter arrived from this man, in which he apologised for what he had previously written.

I could have spent those two years in anger and bitterness, ending up in goodness knows what kind of state of heart, but taking the initiative meant that the door of fellowship and relationship remained open, and still does to this day.

First missionary journey

In 1978 an opportunity came for a friend, Philip, and myself to travel to Ghana, Nigeria and Kenya and to minister at various Conferences and Bible Schools. Being the first ministry trip that both of us had ever been on; we embarked on the journey with tremendous excitement.

We had such a wonderful and blessed time in Ghana, where at the end of the Conference we had the wonderful joy of baptising 200 people in a local river.

It looked so beautiful as we stepped into the river; I should have realised something was amiss as we sank into some sort of gooey mess at the bottom of the river. Of course as you begin to baptise it sort of stirs up the water a little, and what started out as a beautiful clear river ended up a sort of pea-green colour with somewhat of an odour. I was just glad that I was not one of those being baptised.

Coming out of the river and spending time removing the leeches from our legs was not exactly the sort of romantic view that one has of "missionary" work, and certainly not the kind of thing you want to experience on your first trip overseas. Well that was Ghana.

Crisis in the bush

From there we went to Nigeria, where a lot of time was spent teaching in the Bible School at Benin. It was such a privilege, such a joy, to minister to students so hungry for God's Word and with a passion to serve the Lord.

From Nigeria, to Kenya, out into the bush miles from what we would term "civilisation". My travelling companion became ill, with what we realised later was malaria. It got to the stage where he was losing weight, and hallucinating. It is amazing faced with such circumstances the crazy things that go through your mind.

I thought "no one will ever want to travel with me again if he dies. What will I do stuck out here on my own?"

And so I prayed, kneeling down by Philip's bedside seeking the face of God to heal him, not just for his sake but mine. Trying to keep him cool as the fever gripped him even more.

It got to the point one night when he turned to me, as I knelt there praying, and said "Gary, I am going". "WHAT do you mean Philip, you're going?" To which he replied that a man in white had come in a chariot to take him home.

Of course the first thought that comes instantly to your mind is that the Lord has come to take him home.

Brought to remembrance

I thank God for the Holy Spirit. You see, before we had left for Africa the Church had gathered around us to pray God's blessing on the trip. During that prayer time someone had given us a Word of Prophecy.

I didn't remember it all, but in the horror of that moment, the Spirit of God brought back to remembrance not the prophecy but one phrase from that prophecy.

"You shall return in victory" – immediately I said "Philip, what you are seeing is not of God" and so I began to stand against the lies of the enemy, and began to declare over his life the Word of the Lord.

I don't know how long I was praying, but there came a point when Philip turned to me and said, "It's OK now, I can go to sleep". Eventually, after a traumatic journey back to Nairobi, and an even more stressful flight to Israel, we got back to our home in Jerusalem. I remember sitting on a porch with Philip a short time later, as he embarked on a rather lengthy recovery period, and I said to him "Tell me from your point of view what took place".

He reiterated the vision that he had seen while gripped with the fever of malaria. He said "all I had to do was to take the hand of the man who had come for me and I knew I could go home. But the minute you began to stand against the lies of the enemy and quote what God had said, the white robe dropped off and there stood the angel of death." He said that as I continued to pray he felt strength come to him and he began to resist with me until the angel of death left him and he went to sleep.

The joys of the mission field? Well that's debatable, but it certainly reveals the faithfulness of God.

Winter in a place of victory

The good news is that your Valley of Achor, your valley of "trouble" can and will become for you a "door of hope".

Let me put it another way in a Word that was given to me by David Greenow, a very dear friend and one of the most gracious people I have had the privilege of meeting and sharing fellowship with over many years.

"It can't, it won't be winter all the time". In both the natural and the spiritual laws winter always gives way to spring, even though it may be for you a long hard winter, it won't be winter all the time.

Titus 3:12 (NKJV)

When I send Artemas to you, or Tychicus, be diligent to come to me at Nicopolis, for I have decided to spend the winter there.

Paul said, "I have decided, determined, purposed, have made up my mind (*that's a decision*) to winter in a place called Nicopolis". Now the key to this verse is in the name "Nicopolis", it simply means "Victorious City" or "City of Victory".

Paul said, "I have determined to winter in a place of victory". That same determination is the one we all need to make whilst we wait for spring to come.

The Weird, Wacky and Wonderful

One of the weirdest things that I have had to do was whilst we were in Israel. A very dear Sister in the fellowship there, Sarah, was dying of cancer, and to be honest she was just so tired she was looking forward to going home to be with her Master. So much so she had all the arrangements made for her funeral in Jerusalem.

There was one slight problem – she died in Beersheba, in the South of the country, a few days before she was due to come up to Jerusalem.

So we received this frantic phone call, the problem being that having died in Beersheba, she was legally supposed to be buried there quickly.

Sarah's last journey

The result of this phone call was that my wife, who was heavily pregnant, and I were sent down in the dead of night in a Volkswagen "Combi" van to bring her body up to Jerusalem. Apart from the weirdness of this situation, it was also illegal.

So on arrival in Beersheba we placed Sarah's body on the bench seat of the van, and because of the illegal nature of what we were doing, we covered her with clothes, as we had to go through several army check points on our way back to Jerusalem. Her discovery would have meant a shift from Bible teaching to a "prison ministry".

What an amazing 83 kilometre journey back to Jerusalem. Prayer, you talk about prayer, I think our prayer life moved into a whole new dimension on that journey, particularly as we approached each army check point, of which, as you can imagine there were several.

On arrival in Jerusalem, two brothers were posted guards at the top and bottom of the street while we whisked the body from the van to her coffin, which was in the house. I love missionary work!

A slip of the tongue

At one point in my life I was part of the Leadership Team of a large church in England. We had purchased a large building, which had needed a great deal of alteration to convert it from a factory to a church.

But the day of the opening had finally arrived, and as usual there was a certain amount of panic as last minute things needed to be done.

The Senior Pastor had decided at the last minute that he wanted a number of clocks put up in the foyer showing the times in different parts of the world. Someone was rushed off to purchase a number of these clocks; someone else assigned to make up the signs of the different countries.

Eventually they were all in place to his satisfaction, when he realised that some batteries were the order of the day. So he declared to those assembled "Someone needs to go and get some of those 'Durex' batteries".

Of course, as you can imagine, we all fell about in fits of laughter. Blissfully unaware of what he had said, he repeated his plea, and added, "This is no time to joke around, someone needs to go and get some of those 'Durex' batteries."

I suppose the best humour is when we are not trying to be funny, this was certainly the case with our Senior Pastor.

REALLY weird and wacky ...

You see in every church there are people (*bless their cotton socks*) who, whenever opportunity presents itself, will come to the front to "share" what "God" has shown them. Many of them are just "thrown out" without thought or explanation to make of what you will. **These are but a few: -**

♦ There was a man in Africa who stated that he attended a Lutheran Church because he so admired the civil rights leader Martin Luther King.

♦ Pray for Doris she is at death's door, pray that the Lord will pull her through (*Who needs friends like that*)

♦ The Lord has shown me a white flag with a red diagonal stripe.

♦ I have a picture of three flowers, a daisy, a pansy and a chrysanthemum.

♦ The Lord has shown me a vision of two eggs, one hard-boiled and the other fried. The Lord says, "Be not unequally yoked" (*or is it yolked*).

Then there are those who feel out of upset that they have a point to prove. A selection of hurt people who have stood up in a meeting and prophesied to the church that has hurt them.

♦ Thus says the Lord "I am not here"

♦ A dear lady who had been spoken to by the Pastor during the week because of various bits of "gossip" that had been going around the church, and had stormed out of his office. She stood up on the Sunday morning and declared – "I see a sign over the door of this church and it says 'knickerbocker.'" Someone surely should have shouted, "Glory!".

Should it not have been 'Icabod' (*the glory has departed?*) Ah well, in fits of anger we are vulnerable to saying things wrong.

♦ "Thus says the Lord, as I was with you in power on Sunday morning, as I was with you in power on Sunday night, as I was with you in power in the prayer meeting on Tuesday, and as I was with you in power on Friday", (*pause*). "Sorry you didn't have a meeting on Friday." (The "all-knowing" God must have had a memory lapse.)

♦ A statement made by a Pastor in N. Ireland to a rather 'long-winded' preacher. "My brain can only absorb what my backside (*butt*) can take."

"Fire, Fire!"

The senior Pastor of a church in Belfast, N. Ireland had asked his young assistant to preach his first Sunday evening Gospel service. This young man had just finished reading a book on Public Speaking and was eager to try out some of the suggestions.

It so happened that the chapter he had read last was entitled, "How to grab your Audience's Attention". His subject that Sunday evening was on Hell. So wanting to get their immediate attention he thought up a cunning plan!

When he stood up that evening to preach, he looked his congregation straight in the eye and dramatically paused for a few moments. Then cupping his two hands to his mouth he shouted at the top of his voice, "FIRE, FIRE!"

But before he got to finish his sentence an elder jumped up from the back, with a fire extinguisher in his hand, ran up the aisle of the church shouting, "WHERE? WHERE?"

Once the congregation realised what had happened they simply cracked up. The whole place was in fits of laughter, hardly the desired effect for such a solemn subject. I think the young preacher got rid of the book.

Who is mad?

Several years ago a well-known Northern Ireland evangelist was holding a crusade in the city of Armagh. One night after the meeting was long over and the people had gone home, the evangelist and his wife were putting the lights out ready to vacate the premises.

Just then a gentleman walked into the hall and asked for the evangelist by name. When he identified himself the man smiled broadly and produced a letter. Asking the evangelist to read it, he stood and grinned looking rather pleased with himself.

When the evangelist looked at the letter he noticed that the letter-headed paper was from a local mental institution.

The letter stated that the same gentleman had been recently released back into society with a clean bill of health.

When the preacher gave him his letter back the man said, "Now Sir, doesn't that prove that I'm not mad?" Not wanting to upset the man the evangelist replied, "Yes, absolutely, that letter proves indeed that you're not mad".

The gentleman, still smiling broadly, looked him in the eyes, folded up his letter, put it carefully back in his pocket and holding out his hand to the preacher said, "Now Sir, May I see *your* letter?"

The evangelist later said, "I'll never forget the look on his face as he left the building, patting the breast pocket of his coat, as if to say, 'Well, at least I've got my letter!'"

Grand Finale

The baptismal service had been a huge success, the music outstanding and the pianist, conscious of the admiring gaze of the whole congregation played the last bars of the hymn with a flourish, stood to his feet, half-turned and fell headlong into the open and still full baptismal tank.

Revelation

I once had the 'joy' (*loosely translated*) of listening to a man spend twenty minutes relating to the assembled congregation how on a long drive 'God spoke to him' through the various petrol station signs and the 'spiritual' meaning behind them all. As you can imagine we were all 'riveted' about this new revelation.

I will never look at the 'Esso' sign in the same light ever again.

"It was the woman's fault, Lord"

The visiting preacher stood before the congregation, his dress immaculate, immaculate that is until ones gaze arrived at his feet and here the attention of their gaze was arrested by his footwear, a pair of well-travelled and disreputable running shoes. On closer inspection of his personage he also appeared unshaven.

The preacher, very conscious of the surprised and the concealed wonderment of those who sat before him used the situation to his own advantage. "You are no doubt wondering why I should be wearing running shoes this morning? My intention is that your attention should be drawn to the main point of my sermon – Moving on with God."

Inwardly he was smarting at the truth, *my wife forgot to pack my shoes and shaver!* Oh by the way, that visiting preacher was ME!

Demonology

I was involved in a Convention in the States with a number of "big-name" preachers. This particular night I was part of the platform party whilst one of the other ministers preached, and we were to be available to minister at the end of his sermon.

During this brother's message one of the other ministers whispered to us all "did you see that?" Well to be honest I didn't see anything, whatever "that" was. After several more "did you see that" and "there it is again", everyone on the platform saw "that" but me! Well whatever "that" was you must have needed to be on a higher spiritual plane to see it, which obviously I wasn't.

Well apparently they were seeing someone that was "demon possessed" on the left-hand side of the auditorium.

So when the sermon was over and the call was made for people who needed prayer to come forward, these dear ministers were "off" attracted to this person like bees attracted to honey. While the poor preacher, who knew nothing of this, and myself, who in their opinion wasn't spiritual enough, prayed for the hundred or so that were in need.

Did this so-called "demon-possessed" man get delivered? The answer from these "giants of faith" was a definite "No", and "Oh", we were told, "it needed more time, and more in-depth ministry".

The lesson that I learned was that the devil will try and do anything to side-track us away from seeing the very real and genuine need in peoples lives being met.

There is much spoken about the subject of demonology, and I am convinced that the devil gets blamed for a lot that is not his doing at all. That is not to minimise the genuine in any way.

So over the years whilst travelling extensively you encounter a lot that comes under that banner. Here are a couple of genuine incidents that have been part of my own experience.

Captives set free

I met with a Pastor and his wife and a lady that they had brought to meet me. This lady's mother was a renowned 'witch' within the particular village and area where they came from in Ghana.

The story goes that this lady's mother had put a spell on her so that if she attended any meeting or anything to do with the Church she would be gripped by tremendous pain. In the spell that was put upon her by her mother she tied a strong rope (*not literal*) around her waist and when she went near anything connected with Christian beliefs she would feel her mother pull tightly on this rope and so be in tremendous agony.

So while we were talking to this lady she began to writhe in pain and cry out holding her waist. The Pastor's wife lifted her top slightly and you could see great fiery red welts beginning to appear around her waist as the spell took its effect.

As we continued to stand together in prayer, taking authority in the Name of Jesus, the pain began to cease and the welts began to disappear until the lady was totally set free from her mother's control.

The second incident took place in Nigeria at the end of the meeting, as some fifty or so people came forward for prayer, when suddenly a rather large man began to scream and maniacally run about the church blaspheming the Name of Jesus.

He slipped and fell near the front of the church. I was not conscious of logically moving towards him but in a moment I was there. I am not the strongest person in the world, but I reached down, grabbed his shoulders and under the Power of God lifted him up off his feet, set him down and began to pray. Again to witness the reality that there is One that is stronger, that Jesus has all power and authority over the power of the enemy, and is able to set people free.

Wind of the Spirit

A team of us had gone to conduct a series of meetings in South Africa (*three meetings a day for ten days*). We had seen the Power of God move in Salvation, and healing. One particular woman was receiving a progressive healing from crippling arthritis. Each day she would testify of something new that she had done that day that she could not do before (combing her own hair for the first time in years, holding her grandchild in her arms for the very first time).

This particular night before the preaching of the Word, a Prophetic Word was given to the assembled gathering that said, "I myself will minister to my people tonight". I have to be honest none of us really understood what that meant, for as far as we were concerned that is exactly what the Lord had been doing.

So after the preaching of the Word and the altar call was given, at least two hundred people came forward for prayer. It was a beautiful still, calm, balmy evening, and as we, the "ministry team" began to move forward to pray for the people, something remarkable happened.

The Wind of God's Spirit began to blow, so much so you could see the ladies' hair and dresses blowing, twice that wind blew across the front of the auditorium, and at the end of the second time everyone was on the floor, including those who "should" have been ministering. People were being saved, healed, baptised in the Holy Spirit and set free where they lay.

Let me say that God graciously uses people, but He is able to do it by Himself, and that night truly He and He alone ministered to His people. To feel the awesomeness of God's Presence in that way was something that had a profound impact on not only my life but also many lives that night.

Our God is an awesome God

One of the interesting events that happened during that Crusade, was that a young girl of about 11 or 12 years of age, was brought for prayer.

This young girl was so bound within herself that she couldn't even look anyone in the eyes, whatever had taken place in her life, she hadn't smiled or laughed for a long time.

I prayed with her and she gently drifted back in the Spirit, and I moved on to assist others in praying for the many who had come to receive.

A little while later I felt someone tug on my jacket, I turned round to see this young girl standing there, looking up at me, I barely recognised her as the same girl, her face was glowing, and she had a smile you would "die for", she was totally transformed.

She held out her hands to me and said, "Pastor what do I do about this?" I looked at her hands, which were glistening and dripping with oil. I said to her, "The first thing you can do, is pray for me, and then go and pray for your family and friends who came with you, and just let the blessing of God flow".

A chorus that has become popular in recent years says, "Our God is an awesome God". I want to say that He sure is, and as we are open to Him, He is able to do exceedingly abundantly above and beyond all we can not only ask of Him, but even think.

Conclusion

Let me begin this conclusion by quoting a few selected portions from a book called "Finishing Well In Life And Ministry – God's Protection From Burnout" by Bill Mills and Craig Parro (published by Leadership Resources International, Illinois, USA). I have personally found this book very helpful, particularly for the situation in which I have recently found myself.

Burnout

"God has a way of surprising us, bringing circumstances and crises into our lives that are unexpected and which have unpredictable consequences."

"Burnout is primarily an 'inner disease', yet it is often stimulated or exacerbated by outside influences. Ministry disappointment can easily turn into burnout as co-workers and others fail us, or as growth doesn't happen as quickly as we expect. In addition, the larger culture in which we live can also wear on us, draining us of energy and hope: a perfect precursor to burnout."

It has often been said in times of crisis – "There is light at the end of the tunnel". Well I want to say that there is NO light at the end of the tunnel! That's encouraging isn't it? There is light IN the tunnel. Jesus said: -

Hebrews 13:5 (NKJV)

I will never leave you nor forsake you.

Even one of the Names of God is Jehovah Shammah – "The Lord is there". Where is THERE? Wherever you are He is, and yet so often we feel the Lord has forsaken us, that we are on our own. But He is there – it's just that we have taken our eyes off Him, or lost sight of Him.

Psalm 46:1 (NKJV)

God is our refuge and strength, A very present help in trouble.

So when you come to the place of "How long?" and "Why?" – or even to the place of saying, "Where are you God?" – His voice, His Word comes and says "PRESENT help".

Yet I will rejoice

So what happens when through illness and subsequent depression, it seems like all you have known for years has crumbled beneath your feet?

When destiny becomes desperation. When you lose all confidence, when in spite of everything that has taken place, and no matter how many kind things are said about you or even what God has graciously done in and through your life, all you feel is a sense of failure.

When you find the clear distinction between friends and acquaintances. When one of these 'acquaintances' comes to you and makes the comment, "What has happened to you is of great comfort to me, because now I know you are human after all", with the implied sense of "Now you've fallen off your pedestal".

When a chapter closes, and door after door shuts, and yet you cling on to the hope of a new day, a new chapter, a new door.

So where does it leave you?

It leaves you leaning on your faith, leaning on the God you have sought to serve, and you come back to the place that Habakkuk came to.

Habakkuk 3:17-19 (NKJV)

Though the fig tree may not blossom, Nor fruit be on the vines; Though the labour of the olive may fail, And the fields yield no food; Though the flock may be cut off from the fold, And there be no herd in the stalls; Yet I will rejoice in the LORD, I will joy in the God of my salvation. The LORD God is my strength; He will make my feet like deer's feet, And He will make me walk on my high hills.

In these verses Habakkuk is not talking about the extras, the perks that we love to come our way but he is talking about the basics of life, the necessities for living.

But even in the midst of dearth, a dry barren place, a wilderness experience if you will, the Prophet declares – "Yet I will rejoice in the Lord".

"YET". In spite of the prevalent circumstances, in spite of what my eyes see, in spite of how I feel, in spite of the fact that I think, "It shouldn't happen to a Christian" he declares "I will rejoice". I will or I won't, it is a choice, it is a determination, a decision of the will.

And the "God of Hope" brings hope into your life again in unusual ways, and through very special people. I will bless the Lord at all times.

About the author

Gary Stevenson was born in Belfast, Northern Ireland, in 1950, and born again in 1969.
In 1978 he went to Israel as a missionary for 2 years, and subsequently travelled extensively overseas, ministering throughout Europe, Ghana, Nigeria and Kenya, Australia and the United States.

Gary pastored a church in Australia for a year in 1983, then returned to England, where he is now based, ministering throughout the UK and Ireland, and more recently in Zimbabwe and in south-east Asia, including the Philippines, Hong Kong, Singapore and Thailand.

Further copies of this book can be obtained by contacting Gary via his email address:
gaz.ste@ic24.net